*"...For he who comes to God **must believe** that He is, and that He is a **Rewarder** of those who diligently seek Him". Hebrews 11:6*

I0157697

SPIRITUAL KEYS TO FINANCIAL REWARD

UNDERSTANDING BIBLICAL STRATEGIES THAT PROVOKE FINANCIAL INCREASE.

CHARLES OMOLE

Author: Prosperity Unleashed

SPIRITUAL KEYS TO **FINANCIAL REWARD**

Understanding Biblical Strategies that Provoke Financial Increase

Charles Omole

Author "Prosperity Unleashed"

Copyright © 2014

by Charles Omole

ISBN: 978-1-907095-10-8

Published by:

WINNING FAITH
OUTREACH MINISTRIES

London . New York . Lagos

TABLE OF CONTENTS

DEDICATION

This book is dedicated to all the champions of faith in the Marketplace… It is time to develop a superior infrastructure in the spirit and dominate the Marketplace.

INTRODUCTION

"Listen to the message that God is sending your way house of Israel. Listen most carefully; ***don't take the godless nations as your models.*** *Don't be impressed by their glamour and glitz no matter how much they are impressed. The religion of this people is nothing but smoke. An idol is nothing but a tree chopped down, then shaped by a woodman's axe.......* ***Don't be impressed by such stuff it is useless for either good or evil"*** **Jeremiah 10:2-4 (Message version),**

God says "don't take the Godless nations (World's Economic System) as your models". We have begun to see that those who have the mental and human knowledge are failing; like the "experts" managing the banks in our economies, yet broke them. The Bible says don't take them as your models.

Remember that the Wiseman saw the Star of Jesus when they were busy focusing on heaven, looking at all the stars. It is foolishness to think that the only way to get the latest information is by the Internet and worldly media. Looking unto heaven will give you access to such profound and new information that even the powerful will fear what you carry. As children and ambassadors of God, we need to learn to connect with heaven and not focus too much on the land of our assignment for instructions and guidance.

God's people can survive for 40 years on bread that falls out of the sky. Five thousand people can eat their fill and still have leftovers from a meal of two fish and five loaves of bread.

God's economy refuses the law of scarcity and insists that the impossible can happen. It is the miracle that keeps us all alive, despite our rebellion against God and selfishness in relating to one another.

*Neither **was there any among them that lacked***: *for as many as were possessors of lands or houses sold them, and brought the* *prices of the things that were sold, **35** And laid them down at the apostles' feet: and distribution was made unto every man according as he had need.* **Acts 4:34-35 -** *(KJV)*

*But there **will be no poor among you,** for the Lord will surely bless you in the land which the Lord your God gives you for an inheritance to possess.* **Deuteronomy 15:4 AMP**

So we can see from both the Old and New Testament that God's people can live without Lack or Poverty. But there are conditions.

SO LIVING ABOVE LACK IS NOT FICTIONAL OR IMAGINARY. IT IS REAl IN COD'S KINCDOM.

There are two systems in operation on Earth: The Kingdom of the World system and the Kingdom of God system – *God's way of doing things.* So the battle is between the world system and the kingdom of God system. But Satan is the ruler of the darkness of this world. In order to rule; he (Satan) had to put in place a System that he can control and that can guarantee his outcome.

Built within that World System is a reward structure that only favour those that serve Satan. The World system was not intended to advance God's purpose but that of Satan. Therefore; anyone serving God's purpose CANNOT benefit from the World System Satan has set up.

Before a person became born again, he or she operated in the world system. Most people are primarily educated in how to operate according to the world's way of doing things. When a person becomes born again, he or she is in the world but is no longer a part of the world system.

God has a prescribed system of operation for those who are saved, which is greater and better than the world's. Embedded within this system is a financial reward system that is unique to believers in Christ Jesus. How to access this financial reward system is what this book is about. And like any true spiritual principle, I have spent the earlier chapters laying vital foundations that will guide your understanding. These foundations may seem like digression on my part; but they are necessary and I encourage you to patiently follow the sequence of topical revelation as laid out in this book.

Believers must change systems and become educated in the Word of God to learn how to operate in His Kingdom. Many Christians are trying to live according to the world system when they should be operating in the kingdom of God system. This has led to many being controlled by Mammon.

This book goes behind the scene to reveal the spiritual strategy and steps needed to enjoy financial reward from God. The book reveals the essential pillars of the spiritual system that release financial reward. If you have ever sowed seed and not received any harvest yet. If you say, where is my harvest? If you have been faithful giver, tither and yet still live in poverty or lack; then this book is for you. It will answer all these questions and show you how you can command your harvest to manifest by building a superior infrastructure in the spirit.

As we move towards the consummation of all things; believers will begin to live the Higher Life that Christ promised as we begin to take over the kingdoms of this world for the Lord.

So get ready to be lifted to the top as you learn to possess all that Christ has provided for you through the Cross. You will learn how to live above the systems of this word and live the days of heaven on the earth.

I will see you at the top.

Blessings.

Charles Omole
August 2014

Notes

Notes

CHAPTER 1

TUNING TO HEAVEN'S FREQUENCY

Financial reward is not just about money. It is about control. It is about the influence it can afford you in the Marketplace. That is why a wise man that is poor is ignored and overlooked in the Marketplace (Ecclesiastes 9:16). In many nations, those with the wisdom to lead are never in power. It is the idiotic, confused and clueless that often end up in power.

Why? Truth is, when we seek financial increase as believers, we are not just seeking money in itself; but to give effect to our dominion mandate. We are seeking to take over the kingdom of darkness and replace its influence with righteousness. Every money that believers control is money lost to Satan and his kingdom. It is safe to assume he will not release his grasp easily.

Such an aspiration by believers opens the door to spiritual warfare and supernatural encounters. But sadly many in the Church do not fully appreciate this. They do not understand the fact that money always flow in the direction of spiritual power. Either Godly or satanic, it does not matter; you must possess spiritual power to control the tangible resources of the nations.

In my last book, titled: "Breakthrough Strategies for Christians in the Marketplace"; I explained the Marketplace principles in Ezekiel 28. There is a difference between the Prince of Tyrus that you see physically and the King of Tyrus that you do not see. The King is the one really in charge; but it is the Prince that you and I see daily.

So unless you are able to confront and defeat the King, the Prince will never give way. The King the bible tells us is Satan himself. So there are plenty of invisible battles that must be won before you can flourish in the marketplace.

Being well educated means nothing if you do not have spiritual stature to dominate.

Ephesians chapter six verse twelve states in the Living Bible translation that: *"For we are not fighting against people made of flesh and blood, but against* **persons without bodies**—*the* **evil rulers of the unseen world**, *those mighty satanic beings and great evil* **princes of darkness who rule this world**; *and against huge numbers of wicked spirits in the spirit world".*

Many Christians do not fully understand that the basis for spiritual warfare is not primarily personal. You are not at war with Satan simply because of your personal issues or his attack against your person (although there is always an element of this). You are at war because your Nation (Kingdom of God) has declared war against his nation (Kingdom of Satan).

If you are a citizen of God's Kingdom you are automatically at war with the Kingdom of Satan. For instance, if you are an American citizen and America declares war against China for example. You would automatically be at war with China because you belong to a nation that is at war with China.

So it is for the Kingdom of God. Since God's Kingdom is at war with the kingdom of Satan; and we are citizens of God's Kingdom, then we have no other option – we are inevitably involved in the war with the kingdom of Satan. We have been drafted into war by our citizenship of God's Kingdom.

So we must all know how to fight the good fight of faith in every domain of life and culture.

*"But when the Pharisees heard about the miracle, they said, "He can cast out demons because he is Satan, king of devils. Jesus knew their thoughts and replied, "A divided kingdom ends in ruin. A city or home divided against itself cannot stand. And **if Satan is casting out Satan, he is fighting himself and destroying his own kingdom**. And if, as you claim, I am casting out demons by invoking the powers of Satan, then what power do your own people use when they cast them out? Let them answer your accusation! But if I am casting out demons by the Spirit of God, then **the Kingdom of God** has arrived among you". Matthew 12:24-28* Living Bible (TLB).

In this passage, the Pharisees made an ignorant accusation against Christ; that He was using the power of Satan to cast out devils. But in His response, Jesus stated clearly that Satan has his own kingdom. Then He went on to speak also about the Kingdom of God. So there are two kingdoms; one controlled by Satan and the other by God. And there is a battle raging between the two. Two spiritual kingdoms are at war with one another.

The Bible in Ephesians calls Satan the *"Ruler of the Darkness of this world"* and then states that we are fighting against *"Spiritual wickedness in heavenly places"* (Ephesians 6:12). So where is Satan's headquarters? In the HEAVENLY PLACES. But where is that? To understand this teaching; you need to first know that when God created the earth. He gave an instruction that only man-kind can dwell in it. So even after Satan deceived Adam and Eve and got the title deed to the earth; it did not change the fact that only man-kind can freely operate here on earth.

So Satan has to inhabit/possess/dominate people or earthly living beings to be able to operate freely on earth. This is the basis and reason for demonic possessing or oppression or being demonised (a better translation). But in his raw angelic form; Satan and his demons still need a space to dwell and operate from.

That is what Ephesians call the "heavenly places". The key to understanding the location of this place is to recognise that the Bible teaches that there are more heavens than the one we usually talk about. It is essential you understand this reality.

In Genesis chapter one, the first verse states that *"In the beginning, God created the heavens* [plural] *and the earth"*. So from the beginning we see this revelation that there is more than one heaven. Other passages in scripture confirm this point.

"I know a man in Christ who fourteen years ago—whether in the body I do not know, or whether out of the body I do not know, God knows—such a one was **caught up to the third heaven***. ³ And I know such a man—whether in the body or out of the body I do not know, God knows—* ⁴ *how he was* **caught up into Paradise** *and heard inexpressible words, which it is not lawful for a man to utter"*. 2 Corinthians

12:2-4 (KJV)

Apostle Paul's stated here that the third heaven was also the paradise where God dwells. It will be obvious that if there is a third of something; then there must be a first and second. You cannot have a third without one and two preceding it. That means there must be a first and second heaven.

*"Indeed heaven and the **highest heavens** belong to the LORD your God, also the earth with all that is in it".* Deuteronomy 10:14 (NKJV)

*"He that descended is the same also that ascended up far above **all heavens**, that he might fill all things".* Ephesians 4:10 (KJV)

From these scriptural references; we can again see that there is more than one heaven. As God dwells far above all the heavens; and as Paul confirm it as the Paradise of God; the third heaven is therefore where God dwells. The first heaven refers to the Solar System as we know it.

Then there is a space between the visible first heaven that we know and the invisible third heaven, and the bible calls it "the heavenlies". This is the second heaven beyond the first heaven and Satan and his demons occupy this space while the earth is their domain of operations.

It is from this location that Satan and his demonic spirits wage war on believers in the earth while trying to establish his evil kingdom on the earth. It is also from this location that Satan (just like he did as the Prince of Persia) confronts the messenger angels bringing answers to believers' prayers. My mission in this book is to show you how to neutralise this cunning enemy and enforce your victory through Christ Jesus.

Opposition by Satanic Angels

In Daniel chapter 10, we see how he had set aside a period of twenty one days as a special time of prayer and fasting. This is what many call the "Daniel Fast". He did not give up food completely, but ate only fruits and vegetables; he ate no meat and drank no wine. At the end of the three weeks, Gabriel the arc angel came to Daniel with the answer to his prayers and a revelation from God concerning the future of his people.

"Then he said to me, "Do not fear, Daniel, for from the first day that you set your heart to understand, and to humble yourself before your God, your words were heard; and I have come because of your words. 13 But the prince of the kingdom of Persia withstood me twenty-one days; and behold, Michael, one of the chief princes, came to help me, for I had been left alone there with the kings of Persia". - Daniel 10:12-13

What the Bible is saying here is that the angel said "the first day you began to pray, you were heard and I was sent with the response you seek. But it took me three weeks to get through to you because somewhere between the throne of God and you, I was opposed by satanic angels. I had to force my way through those evil angels".

Hence we can see that the satanic kingdom was located somewhere between the earth and the throne of God. The organisational structure and operations of Satan have not changed.

The concept of demonic entities ruling over cities is not a mere theory as some suppose. They operate through physical civic leaders and officials. I have seen this in operation in my own ministry as I travel from city to city, nation to nation. I have learned that to be effective in ministry in a certain city I often must first identify the particular satanic power that is at work in that city. These are called 'territorial spirits' and they are different from city to city. There are many sub groupings within each territory as well, that are controlled by sub-ranks of demonic angels.

So we have to take on the whole armour of God as stated in Ephesians 6 from verse 13. There are seven armours mentioned in Ephesians chapter 6. I will advise that you read that chapter of the bible and familiarise yourself with these armours. Armed with these armour, you then need to "Bind the Strongman" over each city or situation. Explaining these in details is beyond the scope of my goal in this book. But I hope enough have been explained as foundation to help you comprehend the principles in the coming chapters.

Notes

Notes

CHAPTER 2

ANGELS ON REWARD ASSIGNMENT

To understand the spiritual keys to financial reward; you need to be fully conversant with the works and ministry of Angels. Everything God does on earth, He uses Angels as His messengers. Take the story of Daniel for instance. All Daniel was praying for was Understanding. He wanted understanding of the things he had read in the books about the change in season about to come on his people.

I do not intend to do a detailed study into angelic ministry in this chapter; but I will endeavour to give you enough of a snapshot of their operations that will enable you to appreciate their role in enforcing God's covenant on the earth.

God could simply have spoken in heaven; "Receive the understanding son" to Daniel and he would have immediately received it. But what did God do? He sent an angel. This shows you that angels are God's couriers and you will need them if you are to receive anything from God. Despite this fundamental reality; an average believer is vastly ignorant of the ministry of angels.

This has hindered the ability of many believers to navigate the spiritual realm to download into their lives what God has already released. The universe consists Of TWO dimensions/worlds: **The Unseen** and the **Visible realms**.

Col 1:16 - *For by him were all things created, that are in heaven, and that are in earth, **visible and invisible**, whether they be thrones, or dominions, or principalities, or powers: all things were created by him, and for him*

2Cor4:18 - *While we look not at the **things which are seen**, but at the **things which are not seen**: for the things which are seen are temporal; but the things which are not seen are eternal.*

The truth is, what is unseen is more real than what is visible. All things visible were made out of the unseen realm.

Hebrew 11:3 - *Through faith we understand that the worlds were framed by the word of God, so that things which are seen were not made of things which do appear.*

Don't just live by the visible things around you, we must live by the 'more real' things we know. Spirit beings inhabit the spaces all over the earth. Satan and his demons are all angels created by God to function in heaven. But due to his pride; Lucifer (now Satan) and a large number of angels were expelled from heaven by God.

So Demons are malfunctioning angels. Their primary purpose now is to oppose everything that God is doing and ensure believers do not live in the victory that Calvary have already delivered for them. Hence Satan has a passion to keep believers ignorant of the realities of their redemption. This way, he can sell to them lies and falsehood more easily.

Common ANGELIC Characteristics are:

- Angels are created spirits/ beings.
- They are numerous
- They are immortal
- They are powerful
- They are sexless
- They have different names, such as Arc Angels, Cherubims, Seraphims, Angel of nations etc.

The FOUR KEY WORKS OF ANGELS

1. **THEY HAVE A HEAVENLY MINISTRY.** They worship Jehovah all day long.

Isa 6: 1- 5 - In the year that king Uzziah died I saw also the LORD sitting upon a throne, high and lifted up, and his train filled the temple. ² Above it stood the seraphims: each one had six wings; with twain he covered his face, and with twain he covered his feet, and with twain he did fly. ³ And one cried unto another, and said, Holy, holy, holy, is the LORD of hosts: the whole earth is full of his glory. ⁴ And the posts of the door moved at the voice of him that cried, and the house was filled with smoke. ⁵ Then said I, Woe is me! for I am undone; because I am a man of unclean lips, and I dwell in the midst of a people of unclean lips: for mine eyes have seen the King, the LORD of hosts.

Rev 5:11 – 13 - *And I beheld, and I heard the voice of many angels round about the throne and the beasts and the elders: and the number of them was ten thousand times ten thousand, and thousands of thousands; ¹² Saying with a loud voice, Worthy is the Lamb that was slain to receive power, and riches, and wisdom, and strength, and honour, and glory, and blessing. ¹³ And every creature which is in heaven, and on the earth, and under the earth, and such as are in the sea, and all that are in them, heard I saying, Blessing, and honour, and glory, and power, be unto him that sitteth upon the throne, and unto the Lamb for ever and ever.*

Rev. 8:3-4 – *And another angel came and stood at the altar, having a golden censer; and there was given unto him much incense, that he should offer it with the prayers of all saints upon the golden altar which was before the throne. ⁴ And the smoke of the incense, which came with the prayers of the saints, ascended up before God out of the angel's hand.*

They not only worship God, but they take our worship to God. Angels can be the keys to the distance between us and the heaven dimension. They turn our prayers and tears into incense before God. They operate in the heavenly places.

2. ANGELS ALSO HAVE AN EARTHLY MINISTRY.

These angels are committed to the material manifestation of God's will.

An angel showed Hagar the well full of water beside her after God heard the cry of the lad in Genesis 21. They produce the Physical Manifestation of God's Spiritual instructions or will. In the book of Acts; an angel went to deliver Peter from prison.

Angels are the beings that go into action on earth to enforce spiritual declarations of the saints that are in tune with the Word of God. They are programmed to respond to the word of God. They obey the words of God, regardless of whether it was spoken by God or the Believer.

3. ANGELS ARE GODS AGENTS.

The entire scripture is coded into the DNA of

Angels. So they are programmed to obey and enforce the manifestation of God's Word on the earth. They are God's Covenant Enforcement Agents.

Num. 22:24 – " *But the angel of the LORD stood in a path of the vineyards, a wall being on this side, and a wall on that side. [25] And* **when the ass saw the angel of the LORD,** *she thrust herself unto the wall, and crushed Balaam's foot against the wall: and he smote her again".*

Even donkeys know to obey. Balaam would not obey God but the donkey was more sensible that he was.

Mat.13:39 – *The enemy that sowed them is the devil; the harvest is the end of the world; and the reapers are the angels.*

Angels will carry out the judgement of mankind in the last days. Not God himself personally.

4. THEY ARE MESSENGERS.
They are built to be the messengers of God. So what messages do ANGELS carry?

A. **ENUNCIATION.** [To Announce or Proclaim. To set forth precisely or systematically]

Luke 1:11 - *And there appeared unto him an angel of the Lord standing on the right side of the altar of incense.¹² And when Zacharias saw him, he was troubled, and fear fell upon him.*

They enunciate to believers.

B. **WARNINGS**. Angels bring warnings.

Like in Sodom and Gomorrah, God sends angels with warning. Sometime they may take the form of humans to deliver this warnings. So we need to be sensitive.

C. **INSTRUCTIONS**. Angels bring instructions for the saints.

Mat.28:2-6 – *And, behold, there was a great earthquake: for the angel of the Lord descended from heaven, and came and rolled back the stone from the door, and sat upon it. ³ His countenance was like lightning, and his raiment white as snow: ⁴ And for fear of him the keepers did shake, and became as dead men. ⁵ And the angel answered and said unto the women, Fear* *not ye: for I know that ye seek Jesus, which was crucified. ⁶ He is not here: for he is risen, as he said. Come, see the place where the Lord lay.*

D. **ENCOURAGEMENT**. ANGELS can be encouragers. They bring comfort.

Acts 27:22-23 - *And now I exhort you to be of good cheer: for there shall be no loss of any man's life among you, but of the ship. ²³ For there stood by me this night the angel of God, whose I am, and whom I serve.*

E. **REVELATION.** Angels reveal things to believers from time to time as instructed by God.

Act.7:52-53 - *Which of the prophets have not your fathers persecuted? And they have slain them which shewed before of the coming of the Just One; of whom ye have been now the betrayers and murderers: ⁵³ **Who have received the law by the disposition of angels**, and have not kept it.*

Rev.1:1 - *The Revelation of Jesus Christ, which God gave unto him, to shew unto his servants things which must shortly come to pass; and he* *sent and signified it by his angel unto his servant John:*

F. **GUIDANCE.** They Guide the Believer.

Acts 8:26 - *And the angel of the Lord spake unto Philip, saying, Arise, and go toward the south unto the way that goeth down from Jerusalem unto Gaza, which is desert.*

The Holy Spirit lives in us and is the primary guide; but he can use angels to provide more direct physical guide if necessary.

G. **ANGELS BRING CHEER AND STRENGTHEN THE BELIEVER.**

They ministered to and strengthen the prophet.

1Kings 19:5 – *And as he lay and slept under a juniper tree, behold, then an angel touched him, and said unto him, Arise and eat.*

They showed up to strengthen Jesus after his fast for 40days

Mat 4:11 - *Then the devil leaveth him, and, behold, angels came and ministered unto him.*

H. ANGELS DEFEND, PROTECT AND DELIVER GOD'S PEOPLE.

Dan.6:22 – My God hath sent his angel, and hath shut the lions' mouths, that they have not hurt me: forasmuch as before him innocency was found in me; and also before thee, O king, have I done no hurt.

Acts.5:19 – But the angel of the Lord by night opened the prison doors, and brought them forth, and said,

2Kings 6:18 – And when they came down to him, Elisha prayed unto the LORD, and said, Smite this people, I pray thee, with blindness. And he smote them with blindness according to the word of Elisha.

Acts.12:8-11 – And the angel said unto him, Gird thyself, and bind on thy sandals. And so he did. And he saith unto him, Cast thy garment about thee, and follow me. 9 And he went out, and followed him; and wist not that it was true which was done by the angel; but thought he saw a vision. 10 When they were past the first and the second ward, they came unto the iron gate that leadeth unto the city; which opened to them of his own accord: and they went out, and passed on through one street; and forthwith the angel departed from him. ¹¹ And when Peter was come to himself, he said, Now I know of a surety, that the LORD hath sent his angel, and hath delivered me out of the hand of Herod, and from all the expectation of the people of the Jews.

I. ANGELS ARE EYEWITNESSES OF THE CHURCH AND THE BELIEVERS. They are assigned to watch everything that we do.

1Timothy 5:21 *- I charge thee before God, and the Lord Jesus Christ, and the elect angels, that thou observe these things without preferring one before another, doing nothing by partiality.*

1Cor 4:9 - *For I think that God hath set forth us the apostles last, as it were appointed to death: for we are made a spectacle unto the world, and to angels, and to men.*

J. ANGELS GUARD THE ELECT DEAD. Angels know where every Body is, including the dead ones.

Angel Michael watched over the body of Moses for instance.

Luke16:22 – *And it came to pass, that the beggar died, and was carried by the angels into Abraham's bosom: the rich man also died, and was buried;*

Mat 24:31 – *And he shall send his angels with a great sound of a trumpet, and they shall gather together his elect from the four winds, from one end of heaven to the other.*

Jude 9 - *Yet Michael the archangel, when contending with the devil he disputed about the body of Moses, durst not bring against him a railing accusation, but said, The Lord rebuke thee.*

Angels know where all bodies are. Every piece of it. Even if it is mutilated.

K. ANGELS WILL ACCOMPANY CHRIST AT HIS SECOND COMING.
They are coming to earth with Christ

We will see the son of man coming in the cloud of glory with His Angels.

Mat 25:31 - *When the Son of man shall come in his glory, and all the holy angels with him, then shall he sit upon the throne of his glory:*

They will be visible globally at the same time. They will be in their pure, true angelic forms

2Thess. 1:7-8 - *And to you who are troubled rest with us, when the Lord Jesus shall be revealed from heaven with his mighty angels, ⁸ In flaming fire taking vengeance on them that know not God, and that obey not the gospel of our Lord Jesus Christ:*

Angels on Assignment
The angels will implement the judgements of God on the earth. They will apply the judgements of God.

Believers should be more aware of the angelic ministry and their mandate. As we examine the spiritual keys to financial reward there is a vital role for angels as God's messengers. These are not visible matters; but the underlying invisible realities that determine the outcome of our spiritual experiences.

Every time you speak, just bear in mind that Christ as the high priest of our confession hears what we say; but angels also hear what we say and are waiting to be let loose to bring your words to pass. God despatches an angel with the response; just like He did with Daniel. Also the fact that you have not yet received what you prayed for does not mean God has not sent it. You may just need to conduct an effective spiritual warfare (like Daniel) to enforce the manifestation of what God has already released.

In Daniel's case, this time gap was twenty one days; but in your case it could be twenty one seconds, minutes, hours, weeks, months or years. This is just a representative timeline. The key principle here is that there will always be a time lap (no-matter how small) between God releasing something you asked for and you seeing it in physical manifestation in your life.

Understanding the underlying spiritual scenarios, equips you to fight a good warfare. This is why the Bible says we should not be ignorant of the devices/schemes of the enemy in **2 Corinthians 2:11:**

"Lest Satan should get an advantage of us: for we are not ignorant of his devices". KJV

"So that we would not be outwitted by Satan; for we are not ignorant of his designs". ESV

So the more aware of these underlying schemes and methods of satanic opposition we are; the more we can enforce our victory in Christ Jesus.

Principle of Overwhelming Harvest

The Lord stated in the bible that as long as the earth remains, seedtime and harvest will never cease; (Gen. 8:22). The bible also states that the word of the Lord will never return to Him void. That it must accomplish all that He has declared. (Repeated for emphasis).

"So shall My word be that goes forth from My mouth; **It shall not return to Me void,** *But it shall accomplish what I please, And it shall prosper in the thing for which I sent it".* Isaiah 55:11

If these scriptures are true; then for every seed you have ever correctly sown; there is a harvest. "But I still have not received my harvest" some may say. Yes that may be true; but the fact that you did not receive your harvest does not mean God did not release the harvest. There is a difference between God releasing the harvest or response (as Daniel found out) and you receiving what God released.

So what happened to all your harvests that were released but never received by you? As they will not return to God void, they are all still in existence hanging in the heavenly places ready for you once you develop the stature to win in the spiritual warfare. Your harvest is not lost, praise God. You just need to build a superior infrastructure in the spirit. I will be explaining this in more detail in the next chapter.

But to help you understand this vital principle; let me use another biblical story as further illustration. This is the story of the city called Nineveh in the book of Jonah. God spoke to Jonah the prophet that He was going to destroy Nineveh because of their iniquity. In the end after many events, Jonah got to Nineveh; delivered the message God sent him with; that the city will be destroyed.

The Bible states that immediately the entire city repented, led by their king. As a result of this repentance, Nineveh was not destroyed. So the question is; did the word of the Lord to destroy the city return to Him void, not accomplishing what was declared? The Bible already states in Isaiah 55:11 that every word spoken by God MUST accomplish what God declared. But in Jonah we seem to have a situation where the words of the Lord did not accomplish as the city was spared.

But as a good student of the Bible, you will see later in the book of Nahum, chapters 2 and 3 that when a new generation emerged in Nineveh that went back on the repentance and sinned against God. The city was eventually destroyed according the word of Jonah the prophet.

So what happened? When God said that the city would be destroyed, that was like sending a guided missile heading for Nineveh. When the city repented; the missile stayed in the atmosphere but did not detonate. So the city was spared; but the word spoken by God still DID NOT return to Him. God's spoken words NEVER returns to Him. So the 'missile' stayed over Nineveh and would have remain inactive for ever if the city continued to live righteously. But when a new generation came later that went back against God (and started living a life of sin that prompted God's judgment in the first place), the 'missile' that was inactive became active destroying the city as the judgment against sin which was originally spoken by God. So the fact that something has not yet happened does not mean it does not exist.

Similarly, as God's word (that states that there is a harvest guaranteed for every correctly planted seed) will not return to Him void, there is a harvest for every correct seed you have ever sown. Like the missile over Nineveh, they are hanging in the heavenly places, ready for the time you will pull them all down through successful spiritual warfare.

As the story of Job reveal; Prosperity and success will always attract satanic attention and interest. And as he is a devourer; he will be gunning for such a believer. Hence, God has to prepare you for what He has prepared for you.

You will need to attain a certain level of spiritual stature before a certain level of spiritual blessing and prosperity is made manifest in your life. Why? So that you will have what it takes to deal with the devourer when he shows up. This is the reason why the bible says, the blessing of the Lord it makes rich and adds no sorrow to it. There will be no sorrow because God makes sure you have the spiritual firepower (stature) to deal with the devourer before He allows the release of certain level of blessing.

But do not assume this is simply in the hands of God. After He releases your blessings, He does not take it back. But you can be deprived of these 'released' blessings in reality if you have not developed the spiritual stature to overcome the "Prince of Persia" that will inevitably oppose the messenger angels bringing the response to you.

So, if you will obey the Bible (by building a superior infrastructure in the spirit) and act based on the revelation in this book; you can download all your harvests that have been released but not yet manifested; all in one go. That is why the Bible states that when the Lord brought back the captives of Zion, we were like them that dream (Psalm 126:1). All your Captive harvests must be released and will be release in

Jesus mighty name. You will encounter supernatural harvest today in Jesus name. This is what happens when at certain times in your life it seems all you have ever prayed for that seemed delayed all began to manifest and happen at the same time.

When the LORD brought back the captive ones of Zion, We were like those who dream. Ps.126:1 (NASB)

As this is not a book with a focus exclusively on angelic ministry; I advise that you do more study on this issue personally to enhance your understanding of these crucial messengers. I feel it is important to address this topic as part of laying the correct foundation for you to appreciate the operations of the spirit that leads to receiving financial reward.

Notes

CHAPTER 3

SPENDING FROM GOD'S POCKET

It is essential that you and God are on the same page when it comes to financial matters before you can enjoy His financial reward. The earth is the Lord's and the fullness thereof. Consequently when God speaks of financial reward, He is not just referring to Cash. To spend from God's pocket, you must be able to access invisible currency. An exclusive obsession with cash is a main cause of lack and poverty.

Contrary to what the enemy has propagated; in life nobody needs cash. What you need is what cash can buy. Hence, money is defined as a medium of exchange. That means money is what two people agree it is. When Jacob agreed to serve Laban for seven years for each wife;

that labour for seven years became currency. Money is what you have, that is exchangeable for what you need. Cash is the lowest expression of money and as a believer you need to understand that the greatest money available to you is called FAVOUR. Favour does not require an academic qualification. It does not depend on your country of origin, your colour or your contacts. With favour, you can access anything you want even if you have zero in your bank account. That is why the bible says that a good name is better than silver and gold. Why? Because you can exchange a good name for what you need at any time.

So money is not the same thing as cash. If you don't know what money is, you will not know or recognize it when you see it. Cash is a form of Money; but Money goes way beyond Cash. Like I said before, Jacob served 14yrs with Laban for his wives. He paid, but not with cash. Even Words can be Money; Exchanged Goods/services can be money.

Satan controls Cash and he holds on to it very tightly. So God as the creator of the universe, demonstrates His superiority by making us spend from His pocket which does not require cash.

The king's heart is in the hand of the LORD, as the rivers of water: he turneth it whithersoever he will. Proverbs 21:1

When God turns the hearts of kings in your direction; that is favour in operation. And to live a life of perpetual favour, you need to build a superior infrastructure in the spirit. You need to live a life compelling and conducive to the grace that command resources.

Like I noted before, what we need is maybe a car, clothes, house, food and so on, but we make the mistake of thinking we must have cash in our pocket before we can get these things. Hence the blind pursuit of cash by many believers. This has brought many into captivity of mammon. This is a fatal error. If I were to lock you inside a house with $1Billion in cash, with no food, drink and no way out; you will be dead in a few weeks despite having such a large amount of cash with you in the house. Hence, it is not the cash that you really need; but what cash can buy. However, cash is not the only currency available to a believer. If we indeed focus on what we need, rather than always asking for the "cash to buy it"; we will begin to see superior manifestations of God's reward. From today, begin to focus on asking God for what you actually need and leave Him to decide how He gets it to you. This way you open the door to favour as God meets your needs through unexpected and unpredictable means.

Building Superior Infrastructure in the Spirit

Favour is outside the control of Satan and if you live based on favour; you will never be a slave to cash and you will become unstoppable to the enemy. But like I stated before, you need to build a superior infrastructure in the spirit.

Generally speaking; the church is acting like a toothless bulldog in the midst of calamities because there is little or no commitment from the people of God to build a superior infrastructure in the spirit to enable them to pick the signals of what the enemy intends to do and frustrate his plans ahead of time. Operating in the realm of this spiritual infrastructure will enable us to see the invisible, hear the inaudible and touch the intangible. This provokes financial reward in the most unexpected of ways.

The key to building this infrastructure in the spirit is the Holy Spirit. Your walk with the Holy Spirit will determine your ability to build superior spiritual infrastructure. Nobody can know or understand the things of God outside of the Holy Spirit.

So we cannot build infrastructure in the Spirit outside of the Holy Spirit. Building a superior infrastructure in the spirit will enable us to know the enemy's strategies before time and thwart his plans.

Some of the reasons why children of God must build superior infrastructure in the Spirit are as follows:
- The things that are made visible around us today are first made possible in the realm of the spirit.
- Any child of God that cultivates the habit of building superior infrastructure in the spirit will not run around seeking for spiritual helps from lesser gods or consult demons and mediums for direction.
- Building superior infrastructure in the spirit will make us outwit the forces of the wicked.

- It enables us to understand that there is a thin line between revelation and divination.

These points will become clearer to you as you progress in this book. So when we speak about money in the Kingdom of God, we are not referring simply to Cash. We are speaking about invisible currency that is accessible to and operated by those that have built a superior infrastructure in the Spirit. Cash is just one of the many manifestations of money in the Kingdom of God. It is usually the least of the channel God uses. But with favour; you will never lack anything. Favour gives you access to God's pocket; where there is unlimited supply and unhindered flow of resources.

I admonish you to grow where it matters (in the spirit) today. As you grow in the things of God, you will increase in your knowledge of God and in your walk with the Holy Spirit; then spending from the pocket of Jehovah becomes easy.

Finally, you need to understand that God is your only rewarder. He merely uses people as vehicles for your blessing. Never contend with people or see people as your source. In fact

Satan uses people as tools to frustrate your reward from God.

UNDERTANDING TYRE & SYDON

We can't fully appreciate these issues in depth without understanding the spiritual principle of Tyre and Sidon. If you read Ezekiel chapters 26 and 27; there were two cities repeatedly referenced; these are Tyre and Sidon. The bible makes it clear in Ezekiel that there is no manner of trade or business you are looking for that you will not find in Tyre and Sidon.

Hence it means that Tyre and Sidon became the representation of the marketplace. So whoever controls Tyre and Sidon controls the marketplace. And whoever controls the marketplace, controls the destiny of nations. The controller of the marketplace also controls the heavenlies; through which the messenger angels will pass to bring your reward. So you need to have a proper context of human opposition, so that you will not just be fighting in the flesh.

So God told Ezekiel in chapter 28, to do two things; to make a proclamation and a lamentation. The first one is against the **Prince** of Tyre from Ezekiel 28 vs 1 and then from verse 11 to make a lamentation against the **King** of Tyre. We need to understand the differences between these two personalities (the Prince and the King) so that as we proceed we begin to decode the spiritual operations of the Marketplace.

"The word of the Lord came again unto me, saying, ² Son of man, say unto the prince of Tyre, Thus saith the Lord God; Because thine heart is lifted up, and thou hast said, I am a God, I sit in the seat of God, in the midst of the seas; yet thou art a man, and not God, though thou set thine heart as the heart of God: ³ Behold, thou art wiser than Daniel; there is no secret that they can hide from thee: ⁴ With thy wisdom and with thine understanding thou hast gotten thee riches, and hast gotten gold and silver into thy treasures: ⁵ By thy great wisdom and by thy traffick hast thou increased thy riches, and thine heart is lifted up because of thy riches: ⁶ Therefore thus saith the Lord God; Because thou hast set thine heart as the heart of God; ⁷ Behold, therefore I will bring strangers upon thee, the terrible of the nations: and they shall draw their swords against the beauty of thy

wisdom, and they shall defile thy brightness. [8] They shall bring thee down to the pit, and thou shalt die the deaths of them that are slain in the midst of the seas. [9] Wilt thou yet say before him that slayeth thee, I am God? but thou shalt be a man, and no God, in the hand of him that slayeth thee. [10] Thou shalt die the deaths of the uncircumcised by the hand of strangers: for I have spoken it, saith the Lord God. **Ezekiel 28:1-10**

While examining the twin cities of Tyre and Sidon, we need to understand the principles involved. From verse one of Ezekiel 28 the bible tells us that the word of the Lord came to Ezekiel saying "*son of man, say to the* **Prince** *of Tyre thus says the Lord God, because your heart is lifted up, and you say I am God, I seat in the seat of God in the midst of the seas and yet you are a man and not a god*". That instantly means that the prince of Tyre is a human being like you and I. We can also see from verses 2 to 10 of Ezekiel 28 that the prince of Tyre is a human being, that means somebody you can see face to face.

After he made that declaration, God told him that he must now make a lamentation against the King of Tyre, from verse 11. But who is the king of Tyre? As with any kingdom we know; the real decision maker and ultimate power is the King. So the prince can only function to the extent that the King gives him power. Accordingly the real decision maker is the King and not the Prince. So who is this King of Tyre that spiritually controls the Marketplace?

11 Moreover the word of the Lord came unto me, saying, 12 Son of man, take up a lamentation upon the king of Tyre, and say unto him, Thus saith the Lord God; Thou sealest up the sum, full of wisdom, and perfect in beauty. 13 Thou hast been in Eden the garden of God; every precious stone was thy covering, the sardius, topaz, and the diamond, the beryl, the onyx, and the jasper, the sapphire, the emerald, and the carbuncle, and gold: the workmanship of thy tabrets and of thy pipes was prepared in thee in the day that thou wast created. 14 Thou art the anointed cherub that covereth; and I have set thee so: thou wast upon the holy mountain of God; thou hast walked up and down in the midst of the stones of fire. 15 Thou wast perfect in thy ways from the day that thou wast created, till iniquity was found in thee. 16 By the multitude of thy merchandise they have filled the midst of thee with violence, and thou hast sinned: therefore I will cast thee as profane out of the mountain of God: and I will destroy thee, O covering cherub, from the midst of the stones of fire.

[17] Thine heart was lifted up because of thy beauty, thou hast corrupted thy wisdom by reason of thy brightness: I will cast thee to the ground, I will lay thee before kings, that they may behold thee. [18] Thou hast defiled thy sanctuaries by the multitude of thine iniquities, by the iniquity of thy traffick; therefore will I bring forth a fire from the midst of thee, it shall devour thee, and I will bring thee to ashes upon the earth in the sight of all them that behold thee. [19] All they that know thee among the people shall be astonished at thee: thou shalt be a terror, and never shalt thou be any more. **Ezekiel 28:11-19**

Remember verses 1 to 10 was about the prince of Tyre and from verse 11 is the king of Tyre. The Bible stated *"...you are the seal of perfections, full of wisdom and perfect in beauty. You are in Eden the garden of God and every precious stone was your covering, the sardius, topaz and the diamond, the beryl, the onyx, the jasper, the sapphire, the emerald and the carbuncle, and gold, the workmanship of your timbrels and of your pipes was prepared for you on the day you were created. You were the anointed cherub covers... I establish you. You are on the holy mountain of God. You walked back and forth in the midst of the stone you are perfect in your ways from the day you were created until iniquity was found in you..."* So who is the king of Tyre? **Satan is the King of Tyre.**

The prince of Tyre is a human being you see face to face in the marketplace. Who is the prince of Tyre? Anyone that is not born-again and operating in the Marketplace is a prince of Tyre. Nature abhors vacuum so if you are not under the influence of God you must be under the influence of Satan. Hence, anyone you meet in your day to day activities; your boss, your business partner, your colleague; anyone in your workplace that you see around, they are all princes of Tyre if they are not Born Again.

The real controller of the marketplace is the King of Tyre. He (the king of Tyre) is the real controller and the prince of Tyre is just a human being that is being used as a vessel to execute the king's desires. Why? Because when God created the earth; He declared that the only person that can operate legally in it is somebody born of a woman. Satan knows that, therefore he knows that he cannot operate freely without human helpers (Princes). Demons therefore rarely operate on earth outside the human vessels they occupy or dominate to carry out their wishes.

So Satan influences people and he uses people to achieve his objective. The Prince is a physical ruler over Tyre and Sidon (the Marketplace) and the King; Satan is the spiritual ruler. The physical ruler is whom you see but the spiritual ruler is the one pressing the unseen buttons. So we know that the physical ruler is not really your enemy, it is the spiritual one that is your enemy. When there is an issue rather than struggling with the physical ruler, you need to go to where it matters and dislodge the spiritual ruler. Suddenly, the physical ruler becomes easy to deal with. Hence, we wrestle not against flesh and blood.

Therefore the people that are opposing you are doing so, not by themselves, but under the influence of the King of Tyre. It is the King of

Tyre that is using them to oppose you by proxy. Therefore, if you now descend into flesh and blood; (physical fighting), you have missed the point all together. Because it is not about somebody dislike of you, or opposition to you and so on. The issue is, who is controlling that person? And until you understand that there is spiritual warfare going on, you will not succeed in enforcing the manifestation of your harvest.

A typical example was a personal situation a many years ago. I just came back from a trip to the US and my wife (on my return home) gave me a piece of paper; on it she had written a petition, complaining that her boss at work was making her life hellish. And she believed it was racially motivated and so she had written a petition which she wanted me to proof read. I knew instantly that was not the way to handle this.

So I sat her down and explained Ezekiel 28 to her; and I asked that if she wrote a petition, who was she going to give it to? She said their overall boss. I laughed. I thought to myself; *"you are trying to force change on a prince of Tyre; and you are giving another prince of Tyre the opportunity to adjudicate"*. What type of judgment will you get? I said to her that we have to deal with this situation in a different way. So I asked for the name of her manager at work; and I took the case to the Throne Room of God.

About a week later she came back from the office and said, guess what happened? I said, what? She said excitedly that their overall boss came to their office and told her manager (the one giving her stress) that there is a position in another division and that he (the overall boss) had already volunteered this manager for that assignment. My wife's troublesome manager insisted she did not apply for a transfer; but the overall boss said he had already applied on her behalf and she must resume in the new division that same week. That day was the day the woman stopped being my wife's manager.

I then asked my wife, *"how long did you think your petition would have taken to obtain a positive outcome?"* She was ecstatic and that was the end of her problem at work. I dealt with the issue where it matters; rather than resorting to fleshly means. Sadly many believers tend to begin to fight and struggle and by the time we are fighting in the flesh, we are fighting with weapons the enemy control. But if you fight through divine means, Satan does not know what to do with you.

It is therefore important for you to understand that when people are opposing you physically, it is not them. The truth is if you are doing a menial job or are at the lower end of the corporate ladder, or just starting a small business that has next to zero growth possibility; then the enemy may probably not trouble you as much (although you will still have your battles to fight).

But as you begin to climb up in life, you begin to encounter more resistance, in all manners or forms. You need to know how to deal with them, because if you deal with them in the flesh, you will never win. You need to understand that our battle is primarily spiritual. Mammon is a spiritual entity, which we cannot just dip into anyhow.

I read somewhere a while ago that the rate of business failure in the Christian community is the highest. Why? Partly because believers tend to be more trusting in an untrustworthy business climate. But mainly it is because our people stumble into business thinking it is about business plan, some academic qualifications they have and the formula they have read about; but they quickly realize that it is not that easy because Satan will make sure it is not easy for them. You must know that once you are a child of God, Satan has your number. It is not in his interest to make it easy for you.

The bible says in the book of Hebrews 11:29, that *"the children of Israel walked on the red sea as unto dry land. But when the Egyptians tried to do the same, they drowned".* So what does that mean? It means that there is a technology God revealed to his own people, but that technology works only on the platform of relationship. Hence those who see what you do and try to copy the same thing; will not get same result even though they are doing exact the same thing you are doing. Why? Because they don't have a relationship with God that will create the platform or the enabling environment and grace for that thing to work.

Similarly, it works with the enemy too in that he will make certain things in the marketplace easier for his own people but will raise strong opposition against the child of God. Hence the need for spiritual warfare.

Notes

CHAPTER 4

OVERCOMING UNBELIEF

God invites us to ask for big things!

"I am the LORD your God, Who brought you out of the land of Egypt; **Open your mouth wide, and I will fill it".** **Psa. 81:10**

"Call to Me, and I will answer you, and **show you great and mighty things,** *which you do not know."* **Jer. 33:3**

God exhorts us to call on Him so He can give *"great and might things ...."*

Job 37:5 *states that 'God thunders marvellously with His voice; He does* **great things** *which we cannot comprehend'.*

The Psalms then declares in chapter 126 **verse** 3 that *'The LORD has done **great things** for us, And we are glad'*.

So, God desires to do **great things** -- He did for Gideon; for Samson; for Elijah; for Elisha; for Moses; for Joshua; for Hezekiah; for Daniel; for Peter; for Paul and many others. He desires same for you.

God is not a man, that he should lie; *neither the son of man, that he should repent: hath he said, and shall he not do it? or hath he spoken, and shall he not make it good?* **Num. 23:19**

Why have we not experienced the great things promised by God in our lives, especially in our finances?

"The next day, when they came down from the mountain, a large crowd met him. 38 A man in the crowd called out, "Teacher, I beg you to look at my son, for he is my only child. 39 A spirit seizes him and he suddenly screams; it throws him into convulsions so that he foams at the mouth. It scarcely ever leaves him and is destroying him. 40 I begged your disciples to

drive it out, but they could not. ⁴¹ "You unbelieving and perverse generation," Jesus replied, "how long shall I stay with you and put up with you? Bring your son here.

⁴² Even while the boy was coming, the demon threw him to the ground in a convulsion. But **Jesus rebuked the impure spirit, healed the boy and gave him back to his father. ⁴³ And they were all amazed at the greatness of God.**

While everyone was marveling at all that Jesus did, he said to his disciples, ⁴⁴ "Listen carefully to what I am about to tell you: The Son of Man is going to be delivered into the hands of men." ⁴⁵ But they did not understand what this meant. It was hidden from them, so that they did not grasp it, and they were afraid to ask him about it". Luke 9:37-45 (NIV)

Have you ever wondered why the disciples were not able to heal this boy? After all, they were the same disciples who had previously gone from village to village driving out demons and "healing people everywhere" (Mk 6:13, Lk 9:6).

They weren't rookies; they were **seasoned ministers of the gospel.**

It was because they had been successful elsewhere that they were puzzled when they failed on this occasion: In fact they had been given power to cast out devils; yet they could not deal with this particular demon. Why?

*"And when he had called unto him his twelve disciples, he **gave them power against unclean spirits, to cast them out,** and to **heal all manner of sickness** and all manner of disease".* Matthew 10:1

*"And they went out, and preached that men should repent. And **they cast out many devils,** and anointed with oil many that were sick, and healed them".* Mark 6:12-13

So these disciples have not only been given power over all manifestations of Satan; they have also cast our demons before. So why could they not deliver in the case noted in Luke chapter 9?

Subsequently, the disciples came to Jesus in private and asked, ***"Why couldn't we drive it out?" (Mt 17:19).***

This is a representative question. People are today asking God similar question. Why have I not experience the Financial Abundance promised in the Scriptures? Why can I not seem to live above debt? Why am I always surrounded by lack, experiencing poverty and need.....etc. Why am I always sick and not healed?

The answer Jesus gave the disciples is worth looking at in detail. His answer was a representative answer for all our similar questions. In response to their question, "Why couldn't we drive it out?" Jesus answered:

"Because of your unbelief..." **(Mt 17:20)**

Jesus rebuked the disciples for their unbelief. We tend to think of faith and unbelief as opposites. But according to Jesus it's possible to have faith and unbelief at the same time. Unbelief is not the opposite of Faith. The opposite of faith is fear. So faith and unbelief that cohabit in a believer leading to paralysis and suspended reward.

As a believer, you don't have a faith problem. You live by the faith of the Son of God, so there can be no problem with your faith. When the disciples asked Jesus to increase their faith; He responded that the size of their faith was not the problem. So faith is not the problem; it is unbelief.

*"And if he trespass against thee seven times in a day, and seven times in a day turn again to thee, saying, I repent; thou shalt forgive him. ⁵ And **the apostles said unto the Lord, Increase our faith.** ⁶ And the Lord said, If ye had faith as a grain of mustard seed, ye might say unto this sycamine tree, Be thou plucked up by the root, and be thou planted in the sea; and it should obey you".* Luke 17:4-6

So Jesus was making them realise that even a tiny faith can move mountains; so faith is not the problem.

*Jesus replied, "I tell you the truth, if you have faith and **do not doubt**, not only can you do what was done to the fig tree, but also you can say to this mountain, 'Go, throw yourself into the sea,' and it will be done." (Mt 21:21)*

"Jesus said to him, "If you can believe,[a] all things are possible to him who believes."

74

[24] Immediately the father of the child cried out and said with tears, **"Lord, I believe; help my unbelief!"** *[25] When Jesus saw that the people came running together, He rebuked the unclean spirit, saying to it, "Deaf and dumb spirit, I command you, come out of him and enter him no more!" Mark 9:22-25*

The father is saying he has faith, but he also has unbelief. Unbelief nullifies faith. In Matthew 13:58 it says (about Nazareth) *"He did not many mighty works there* **because of their unbelief."** Mark 6:5 says, *"Jesus could not do* **mighty works** *there, except to heal a few sick folk,* **because of their unbelief."**

Unbelief in believers is the biggest block to receiving financial reward from God.

"Then the disciples came to Jesus privately and said, "Why could we not cast it out?" [20] So Jesus said to them, "Because of your unbelief; for assuredly, I say to you, if you have faith as a mustard seed, you will say to this mountain, 'Move from here to there,' and it will move; and nothing will be impossible for you.." **(Mt 17:19-20)**

75

After identifying the problem ("your unbelief"), Jesus assured the disciples that their faith was not the issue. Even if their faith was the size of a little mustard seed, it would be sufficient to move mountains.

The real obstacle was **their unbelief.** Jesus called them an *"unbelieving and perverse generation"* (Mt 17:17). He was saying, *"You had faith, but it was undermined by your unbelief."*

Note that some translations interpret "unbelief" as "little faith." So Jesus' answer in verse 20 begins, "Because of your *little faith*." But this is a poor translation that makes Jesus sound like He's contradicting Himself. The Greek word for unbelief (**apistia**) in the passage above is the same word used by the boy's father when he says, "help my unbelief."

The three different kinds of unbelief.

There are usually three sources of unbelief in believers.

1. Firstly, there is unbelief that arises from ignorance (example, "I didn't know God heals the sick"). Ignorance of the word

and lack of knowledge of God's principles can lead to unbelief in Christians. Without the foundation and anchor of the Word, unbelief readily arises.

2. Secondly, there is unbelief that arises from bad theology (example; "I don't believe God heals the sick anymore because I was taught so"). With many Christians growing lazy in personal study of the Word of God; they have relied on their teachers to explain the bible to them. But if these teachers belief wrongly (wrong doctrine); they will teach the wrong things. Hence unbelief can be birth in people based on bad theology.

3. Thirdly, there is unbelief that arises from our natural senses (example is when a person says "look at the size of that tumour!" Such physical sighting can create unbelief due to panic). You are in such instances *now walking by sight rather than faith (2 Co 5:7)*. We may be declaring the promises of God over our situation but at the same time we're feeding our doubts by heeding our circumstances.

Our environment trains us to see the facts. To receive from God, you need to train your heart to see the truth. It is what your heart sees that it believes and it is what your heart believes that you experience.

How do we deal with unbelief?

Starve it! And He replied to them, *"This kind (of unbelief) cannot be driven out by anything but prayer and fasting." (Mk 9:29)*

Unbelief that arises from ignorance and bad theology can be corrected by showing people the Truth (Mk 6:6); But overcoming natural sense unbelief may require prayer and fasting. How are you starving your unbelief? If you are not starving your unbelief; you are feeding it. There is no middle ground.

So check your lifestyle and daily routine. If the Internet is fuelling your doubts, then stay off the Internet! If your "faith sense" is dull because of your natural appetites, then curb your appetites. If your body is telling you what to think and believe ("I'm hurting – I'm not healed at all") then deny your flesh by going without food.

Your flesh needs to learn that it is not in charge – you are! By fasting for a time you are telling your five senses that there's more to life than bread (Mt 4:4); you're saying that you prefer to live by the spirit. But I will explain more on this in the coming chapters.

When it comes to financial reward from God, You don't have a faith problem. What you have is an unbelief problem. Instead of trying to build bigger and bigger faith, we need to rather stop feeding our unbelief.

Today, there is much emphasis on faith and getting more faith. This sort of teaching will leave you thinking, *"I'm not healed because I lack faith."* Like the disciples we pray, *"Lord, increase my faith" (Lk 17:5),* and Jesus responds, *"Your faith is not the problem – even little faith will get the job done"* (Lk 17:6, my paraphrase).

Why is our faith not the problem? Because it's *His* faith. Paul said he was justified *by the faith of Jesus Christ* and we *now lived by the faith of the Son of God* (Gal 2:16,20, KJV).

He understood that his faith was a gift from God

(Eph 2:8). If you think there's something wrong with your faith, it's like saying God gives faulty gifts. When Peter healed the crippled man outside the temple, he gave all credit to the faith that comes from God:

*"By **faith in the name of Jesus**, this man whom you see and know was made strong. It is **Jesus' name and the faith that comes through Him** that has given this complete healing to him, as you can all see." (Acts 3:16)*

When there's a problem, a strategy of the devil is to get your attention on fixing the thing that's not broken. This becomes a distraction.

If Christ lives in you, then there's nothing wrong with your faith. But you might have a problem with unbelief. So before you can enjoy financial rewards from God, you must deal with unbelief. This is why I have taken the time to explain these essential foundational principles.

Notes

Notes

CHAPTER 5

Developing Faith for Abundance

Before we examine the spiritual keys to financial reward; there is one more principle I need to explain to help in your understanding of this subject.

God wants you to prosper in every way, but prosperity, like all things in the kingdom of God, is governed by <u>spiritual laws</u>. There is no prosperity apart from the word of God, so the word must be the basis of your prosperity. The law of the spirit of life in Christ Jesus governs prosperity and supernatural supply and ultimately financial reward.

Prosperity is more than money. The word *prosperity* comes from the Hebrew word *shalom*, which means, *"peace; well-being; wholeness; having nothing missing or broken."* Prosperity is having the ability to meet your needs and that of others, whenever the needs arises.

God desires for you to have total life prosperity (3 John 2). Soul prosperity is when your mind is yielded to the Word of God. There is no true prosperity apart from the Word.

The Law of the Spirit of life in Christ Jesus governs prosperity and supersedes the law of sin and death (Romans 8:2). **When you don't obey laws, you can get hurt.** For example, if you step off of the top of a building, the law of gravity dictates that you will fall to the ground. The force of gravity makes the law of gravity work. To get out from under laws that are working against you, you must begin to operate under a law that is greater or superior.

The law of thrust and lift supersedes the law of gravity. Sickness, poverty, lack and bondage cannot override the law of the Spirit of life in Christ Jesus. You have to learn how to operate at a higher level of existence. You cannot develop faith for abundance and reward if your motive for abundance is ungodly. Hence, you cannot command financial reward from God, if your heart is anchored on greed and materialism. Your motive for financial reward must therefore be right. If you lack an understanding of God's purpose for financial abundance; you will abuse it if released to you. But some will argue by saying but *"I can do all things through Christ who strengthens me"* (Philippians 4:19). What they fail to realise is that God will not strengthen you to do something against His will. Hence your desire MUST still be divine purpose driven.

In the Kingdom of God; Faith causes every law to function. The Word of God must be your base. Spiritual laws will work when they are put to work, but they stop working when the force of faith is not applied. Satan's goal is to convince you that God's Word won't come to pass. He causes you to doubt, which causes your faith to stop working.

Jump-start your faith by getting back in the Word of God. God has already done everything He is going to do; He has put laws in place that will propel you in the corresponding direction of your decisions.

Law of Faith that releases Financial Reward.

Faith for Abundance must dwell in <u>Two Places</u> within you.

*"We having the same spirit of faith, according as it is written, I **believed**, and therefore have I **spoken**; we also believe, and therefore **speak".** 2 Corinthians 4:13*

The above passage shows that if you are going to believe something, it is not complete until you say it. And that if you say something that will work, it must be because you believe it. The two goes together.

*[6]But the righteousness which is of faith <u>speaketh</u> on this wise, Say not in thine heart, Who shall ascend into heaven? (that is, to bring Christ down from above:) [7]Or, Who shall descend into the deep? (that is, to bring up Christ again from the dead.) [8]But what saith it? The word is nigh thee, even in **thy mouth, and in thy heart**: that is, the word of faith, which we preach; [9]That if thou shalt confess with thy*

mouth the Lord Jesus, and shalt believe in thine heart that God hath raised him from the dead, thou shalt be saved. **¹⁰For with the heart man believeth unto righteousness; and with the mouth confession is made unto salvation.** *¹¹For the scripture saith, Whosoever believeth on him shall not be ashamed.* **Romans 10:6-11 (KJV)**

Romans 10:8-10 (AMPLIFIED VERSION)
⁸But what does it say? The Word (God's message in Christ) is near you, on your lips and in your heart; that is, the Word (the message, the basis and object) of faith which we preach,⁽ᴮ⁾ ⁹Because if you acknowledge and confess with your lips that Jesus is Lord and in your heart believe (adhere to, trust in, and rely on the truth) that God raised Him from the dead, you will be saved. **¹⁰For with the heart a person believes (adheres to, trusts in, and relies on Christ) and so is justified (declared righteous, acceptable to God), and with the mouth he confesses (declares openly and <u>speaks out freely his faith</u>) and confirms [his] salvation.**

The mouth speaks out your faith. However, faith for abundance must be in two places in order to work.

- Faith must be in your **Heart** and
- Faith must be in your **Mouth.**

If faith is not in the heart and in the mouth then manifestation of financial reward in the physical realm is not possible. If Faith must be in two places, where does it have to be first; Heart or Mouth? Many believers think it is in the Heart first; but that is not correct.

If I read promises of God from the bible with my mouth; that does not mean I believe it. Because, you read with your mouth in the bible that you have been healed, does not mean you believe it and will experience healing.

*[8]This Book of the Law shall not depart out of **your mouth**, but you shall meditate on it day and night, that you may observe and do according to all that is written in it. For then you shall make your way prosperous, and then you shall deal wisely and have good success.* **Joshua 1:8 (Amplified Bible)**

Faith is first in the Mouth. First mouth, then heart. But how does it get from the mouth to the heart?

*"Let not mercy and truth forsake thee: bind them about thy neck; **write them upon the table of thine heart".** Proverbs 3:3 (KJV)*

You mean Faith can be written into the table of our hearts? Yes it can. But how do you get Faith from your mouth into your heart?

*"My heart is inditing a good matter: I speak of the things which I have made touching the king: **my tongue is the pen of a ready writer".*** Psalm 45:1 (KJV)

My tongue is the pen of a ready writer. Question: How do you write faith into the tablets of your heart?
Answer: By Speaking the Word.

My Tongue is the writing instrument. So, whenever you confess the word of God you are writing it into your heart, and as you persist and continue doing so, it will be established in your heart. And as you continue confessing the word after it has been written into your heart; it will begin to produce physical manifestation.

So you have to first get the word into you, in order to get the word out of you to produce result. Thus the mouth has an entrance and an exit. If you don't speak it you will not believe it and if you don't believe it you will not have it.

The faith that provokes financial reward is a mouth to heart connection. Your heart here means your Spirit Man. In the Garden of Eden, the soil of man's heart was corrupted; so Jesus had to come for us to become Born Again, so that we can be given a new heart; which can now produce good fruit.

Joshua 1:8 (Amplified Bible)

*8This Book of the Law shall not depart out of **your mouth**, but you shall meditate on it day and night; that you may observe and do according to all that is written in it. For then you shall make your way prosperous, and then you shall deal wisely and have good success.*

You must never stop declaring the word; if you don't let it depart from your mouth, it will eventually be written into your heart and that is what produces faith for abundance. **If you continue saying it, your spirit will bring you to it.** So, when it appears that God is not working or it seems to you like heaven is silent; keep saying the word; because you are building faith into your heart by declaring the word. Your spirit man like a good soil will have to germinate the word-seed you have been sowing. This is what produces life. Your Spirit man is the manufacturing centre for life. It is the ground that grows your word seed.

That is why the bible says:
"Keep and guard your heart with all vigilance and above all that you guard, for out of it flow the springs of life". Proverbs 4:23 (Amplified Bible).

So if you don't like how you are living, plant a new crop into your heart. Sometime you don't know how much negatives come out of your mouth daily, until you begin to train yourself to speak right.

"For verily I say unto you, That whosoever shall say unto this mountain, Be thou removed, and be thou cast into the sea; and shall not doubt in his heart, but shall believe that those things which he saith shall come to pass; he shall have whatsoever he saith. [24]Therefore I say unto you, What things soever ye desire, when ye pray,

believe that ye receive them, and ye shall have them". Mark 11:23-24 (King James Version).

That shows me that my prayer life and my confession life has to be consistent. Saying and praying must profess the same thing. They must line up together.

JUSUS SPOKE TO AN 'IT' (A Thing)

Mark 11:12-14 -   *[12]Now the next day, when they had come out from Bethany, He was hungry. [13]And seeing from afar a fig tree having leaves, He went to see if perhaps He would find something on it. When He came to it, He found nothing but leaves, for it was not the season for figs. [14]__In response__ Jesus said to it, "Let no one eat fruit from you ever again." And His disciples heard it.*

In response to what? Who spoke that Jesus responded to? He responded to an "IT". That is, the Fig Tree.

'IT' is an example of a situation. Your situation is talking to you all the time, you must talk back at it. When was the last time you spoke to your "It"? You have to maintain all your

'It' by the word of God in your mouth.

Mark 11:20-24 – "*Now in the morning, as they passed by, they saw the fig tree <u>dried up from the roots</u>. ²¹And Peter, remembering, said to Him, "Rabbi, look! The fig tree which You cursed has withered away."*
²²So Jesus answered and said to them, "Have faith in God. ²³For assuredly, I say to you, whoever <u>says</u> to this mountain, "Be removed and be cast into the sea,' and does not <u>doubt in his heart</u>, but believes that those things he says will be done, he will have whatever he says. ²⁴Therefore I say to you, whatever things you ask when you pray, believe that you receive them, and you will have them".

When you speak the word of faith with the mouth-heart connection, it attacks the root of the problem. You cannot pray wrongly and expect an answer; similarly, you cannot pray right and then confess wrongly after and expect an answer. You have to continue to confess what you have prayed about.

You have to pray and confess the word of God. When you pray the word of God, heaven understands you.

In Mark 11:23; what does the bible say we will have? Whatsoever we SAY. Whatsoever means what you have in your heart. So if I don't have in me what I say, I cannot have it. (From the abundance of the heart the mouth speaks)

I am not going to have what I said, if I did not have it before I said it. Your life cannot become more than your words declares it to be. Faith must be in two places before it can produce results of financial reward. Words are spiritual vehicles. They either carry faith of fear. And the heart is the soil that receives either.

Your heart will grow in faith or fear; depending on the word seed your mouth has planted. In the beginning was the word; hence whatever you want to begin, must begin with your Word. God never does anything without saying it first.

"A fool's mouth is his destruction, and his lips are the snare of his soul". **Proverbs 18:7**

"Death and life are in the power of the tongue: and they that love it shall eat the fruit thereof". **Proverbs 18:21**

"If any man among you seem to be religious, and <u>bridleth not</u> his tongue, but <u>deceiveth his own heart</u>, this man's religion is vain. James 1:26-29

How do you deceive your heart? The tongue knows what is in your heart; because the tongue wrote it there. And your heart (your spirit) assumes that what you speak is what you want. You deceive your heart when you have written something in it by your mouth and then you try to harvest something else with the same mouth at a later stage.

This causes your spirit to LOCK UP so to speak. It is from the abundance of the heart that the mouth will speak; but if you try to speak outside the abundance of your heart; then you are deceiving your heart.

Luke 17:21 (King James Version) - *²¹Neither shall they say, Lo here! or, lo there! for, behold, the kingdom of God is within you.*

Luke 17:21 (Amplified Bible) - *²¹Nor will people say, Look! Here [it is]! or, See, [it is] there! For behold, the kingdom of God is within you [in your hearts] and among you [surrounding you].*

So your heart is the production centre. The raw materials are the words you speak. What are you producing? Faith or Fear. Doubt or Believing. Life or death.

The choice is yours. But Faith that compels financial reward must be in two places before the word can work for you.

Notes

Notes

CHAPTER 6

Keys to Activating Financial Reward

*"But without faith it is impossible to please Him, for he who comes to God **must believe** that He is, and that He is a **rewarder** of those who diligently seek Him". **Hebrews 11:6***

Here in the same sentence; we see God's ability to reward, linked to our Belief. But how do we provoke supernatural financial reward as believers? In this chapter, I will show you the three keys to financial reward. If you will enjoy financial reward in the kingdom of God, you must possess these three keys as a norm in your life.

The FIRST key to financial reward is your Giving.

*"Take heed that you do not **do your** charitable deeds [that ye do not your alms or GIVING] before men, to be seen by them. Otherwise **you have no reward from your Father in heaven.** [2] Therefore, when you do a charitable deed [GIVE], do not sound a trumpet before you as the hypocrites do in the synagogues and in the streets, that they may have glory from men. Assuredly, I say to you, they have their reward. [3] But when you do a charitable deed [GIVE], do not let your left hand know what your right hand is doing, [4] that your charitable deed [GIVING] may be in secret; and your Father who sees in secret will Himself REWARD YOU openly.* Matthew 6:1-4 (Emphasis is mine)

It will not come as a surprise that our giving is a basic requirement for financial reward. Many books have been written on giving and it is a very much understood concept in the Church that you must give before you can get any harvest. So I will not dwell too much on this point.

The SECOND key to financial reward is your Praying.

*"And **when you pray**, you shall not be like the hypocrites. For they love to pray standing in the synagogues and on the corners of the streets, that they may be seen by men. Assuredly, I say to you, they have their reward.* **⁶ But you, when you pray, go into your room, and when you have shut your door, pray to your Father who is in the secret place; and your Father who sees in secret will <u>REWARD YOU openly</u>***. Matthew 6:5-6*

So after you have given; (based on my explanations In Chapters 1, 2 and 3), you kick-start a spiritual chain of activities. During which the devil will oppose your servant angel from bringing the response down to you. Hence, you must initial spiritual warfare through prayer, (just like Daniel).

The THIRD key to financial reward is your Fasting.

*"Moreover, **when you fast**, do not be like the hypocrites, with a sad countenance. For they disfigure their faces that they may appear to*

*men to be fasting. Assuredly, I say to you, they have their reward. ¹⁷ But you, when you fast, anoint your head and wash your face, ¹⁸ so that you do not appear to men to be fasting, **but to your Father who is in the secret place; and your Father who sees in secret will <u>REWARD YOU openly</u>.** Matthew 6:16-18*

So as you can see; Verse 4 (GIVING), Verse 6 (PRAYING), and Verse 18 (FASTING) each ended with exactly the same declaration of Truth… *"Your Father who sees in secret will <u>REWARD YOU OPENLY</u>"*

Therefore these three acts are the Supernatural KEYS to generate supernatural reward from God.

You Give for Increase
You Pray for Increase
You Fast for Increase.

Some may ask how can we be sure this chapter (Matthew 6) is actually about Finances….well …let us continue reading the chapter from Matthew 6: 19 to see what the Bible reveals to us about the focus of this entire chapter?

"Do not lay up for yourselves treasures on earth, where moth and rust destroy and where thieves break in and steal; [20] but lay up for yourselves treasures in heaven, where neither moth nor rust destroys and where thieves do not break in and steal. [21] For where your treasure is, there your heart will be also.

[22] *"The lamp of the body is the eye. If therefore your eye is good, your whole body will be full of light. [23] But if your eye is bad, your whole body will be full of darkness. If therefore the light that is in you is darkness, how great is that darkness!*

[24] **"No one can serve two masters; for either he will hate the one and love the other, or else he will be loyal to the one and despise the other. <u>You cannot serve God and mammon.</u>**

[25] *"Therefore I say to you, do not worry about your life, what you will eat or what you will drink; nor about your body, what you will put on. Is not life more than food and the body more than clothing? [26] Look at the birds of the air, for they neither sow nor reap nor gather into barns; yet your heavenly Father feeds them. Are you not of*

*more value than they? ²⁷ Which of you by worrying can add one cubit to his stature? ²⁸ "So why do you **worry about clothing?** Consider the lilies of the field, how they grow: they neither toil nor spin;²⁹ and yet I say to you that even Solomon in all his glory was not arrayed like one of these. ³⁰ Now if God so clothes the grass of the field, which today is, and tomorrow is thrown into the oven, will He not much more clothe you, O you of little faith?*

³¹Therefore do not worry, saying, 'What shall we eat?' or 'What shall we drink?' or 'What shall we wear?' ³² For after all these things the Gentiles seek. For your heavenly Father knows that you need all these things. ³³ But seek first the kingdom of God and His righteousness, and all these things shall be added to you. *³⁴ Therefore do not worry about tomorrow, for tomorrow will worry about its own things. Sufficient for the day is its own trouble.*

So we can see that this chapter is about Abundance and WEALTH; Hence CHRIST referred to the three Keys that unlocks Supernatural REWARD from God. Your GIVING; your PRAYING and your FASTING.

The fact that your GIVING unlocks supernatural

reward, is not news to many Believers. But many do not know that PRAYER and FASTING is connected to Financial REWARD. This is where many Believers are failing in their quest for financial provision and victory over unbelief.

Why is PRAYER and FASTING essential to financial reward along with your Giving? Because money will always only flow in the direction of spiritual power. Your Giving will command a release from Heaven; but as Daniel found out; Heaven releasing a REWARD does not guarantee you will receive it if you do not back-up your Giving with Spiritual Power. I have explained in the foundational principles earlier chapters why this is the case.

So in addition to your Giving; you have to engage in Spiritual warfare through Prayer and Fasting. Satan is the Ruler of the Darkness of this world and he controls Money as MAMMON Spirit. Because of God's WORD that Seed MUST be followed by Harvest; God releases based on your cheerful giving....BUT Satan will also immediately swing into action.

He will not let go simply because of your giving....He will only let go because of your

superior spiritual Power. Fasting and Praying is also essential in activating the ministry of angels as explained before. In case you skipped the earlier chapters of this book where I explained this in detail; allow me (for emphasis) to summarise the principles briefly here.

Paul had a vision of the 3rd Heaven: 2Cor 12:2-4 The 3rd Heaven is also referred to as the PARADISE and Abode of God. The First Heaven is the Solar System as we know it, including the earth. So WHO occupies the SECOND Heaven? BIBLE states that our Battle is against Spiritual Wickedness in HEAVENLY PLACES. Where is that? (Demons cannot fully operate freely in their bodiless form on earth based on God's law; although there may be occasional appearances. God has stated that the earth was created for man-kind. So Satan and his fallen angel demons need a place to occupy in their raw/original form. Where is that? This is believed to be the 2nd Heaven.

Angels are the MESSENGERS of God to Minister and provide responses to our requests as we saw in Daniel. But as we also saw in Daniel, they MUST Battle through the second Heaven to arrive on earth with our response.

So you must believe that God is a REWARDER. You MUST be a GIVER. You must be PRAYERFULL; then you must FAST. You have to deal with any unbelief in these areas. Now that we understand the THREE Keys of Supernatural Financial Reward; How do we as believers then Dominate in the Marketplace.

Answer to this was the subject of my previous book titled, *"Breakthrough Strategies for Christians in the Marketplace".* I will advise you get a copy. But in order to help bring a sound conclusion to this teaching, I will give a brief summary of the biblical thesis for marketplace dominion in the final chapter of this book.

Notes

CHAPTER 7

THE PURPOSE OF REWARD

The Bible declared in Isaiah 2:2-4 that the *Mountain of the Lord's House shall be exalted at above all mountains...*This refer to happenings in the latter days before the consummation of all things. But how is this going to take place?

"And I saw another mighty angel come down from heaven, clothed with a cloud: and a rainbow was upon his head, and his face was as it were the sun, and his feet as pillars of fire: [2] And he had in his hand a little book open: and he set his right foot upon the sea, and his left foot on the earth, [3] And cried with a loud voice, as when a lion roareth: and when he had cried,

seven thunders uttered their voices. *⁴ And when the seven thunders had uttered their voices, I was about to write: and I heard a voice from heaven saying unto me, Seal up those things which the seven thunders uttered, and write them not.*
⁵ And the angel which I saw stand upon the sea and upon the earth lifted up his hand to heaven,
⁶ And sware by him that liveth for ever and ever, who created heaven, and the things that therein are, and the earth, and the things that therein are, and the sea, and the things which are therein, that there should be time no longer:
⁷ But in the days of the voice of the seventh angel, when he shall begin to sound, the mystery of God should be finished, as he hath declared to his servants the prophets".
Revelation 10:1-7 (KJV)

The Bible states that John heard the Seven Thunders utter their voices after the Angel roared. What did the Seven Thunders say? What are the seven Thunders?

John was instructed to Seal up what he heard, just as he wanted to write down what he heard. And in Verse 7, the Bible says that when the 7th Angel shall sound; All will be revealed.

What Secret was sealed up by John that will be revealed after the seventh angel have sounded? Also has the 7th Angel sounded yet? YES, the seventh ANGEL has sounded already.

Revelation 11:15 -- *15 And the **seventh angel sounded;** and there were great voices in heaven, **saying, The kingdoms of this world are become the kingdoms of our Lord, and of his Christ; and he shall reign for ever and ever**.*

From verse 15; we can see that the 7th ANGEL sounded already and what he said relates to the kingdoms of this world becoming the kingdoms of our Lord. (Reclaim of the marketplace and Nations). So what John was asked to seal up was a revelation about the secrets of the Reclaim of the Marketplace and the nations of the earth for the Lord. So what did John do next? What MUST we do to bring into existence what John heard and sealed.

Revelation 10:8-11 provides more answers.
8 And the voice which I heard from heaven spake unto me again, and said, Go and take the little book which is open in the hand of the angel which standeth upon the sea and upon the

earth. *⁹ And I went unto the angel, and said unto him, Give me the little book. And he said unto me, Take it, and eat it up; and it shall make thy belly bitter, but it shall be in thy mouth sweet as honey. ¹⁰ And I took the little book out of the angel's hand, and ate it up; and it was in my mouth sweet as honey: and as soon as I had eaten it, my belly was bitter. ¹¹ And he said unto me, Thou must prophesy again before many peoples, and nations, and tongues, and kings.*

John was told to *'Eat the book'*. He was then able to declare again to the people only after eating the book. WHAT IS THE IMPORTANCE OF EATING THE BOOK? What is the book? How do we decode the meaning of eating the book? What does this mean?

Jeremiah 15:16 -- *¹⁶ Thy words **were found, and I did eat them; and thy word was unto me the joy and rejoicing of mine heart: for I am called by thy name, O LORD God of hosts.***

Ezekiel 3:1-4 -- ***Moreover he said unto me, Son of man,*** *eat that thou findest; eat this roll, and go speak unto the house of Israel. ² So I opened my mouth, and he caused me to eat that roll. ³ And he said unto me, Son of man,* *cause thy belly to eat, and fill thy bowels with this roll that I give thee. Then did I eat it; and it was in my mouth as honey for sweetness. ⁴ And he said unto me, Son of man, go, get thee unto the house of Israel, and speak with my words unto them.*

Satan is the ruler of the darkness of this world and he currently rules the Marketplace. So any engagement of the Marketplace by a believer is a declaration of war. You are seeking to dispossess him of his spoils. For that to happen you need spiritual power.

You must build superior infrastructure in the spirit. This is required to release into physical manifestation what God has already released. You cannot speak in the Marketplace accurately unless you have EATING the book. YOU MUST HAVE EATEN THE WORD.

Revelation 10:1-3 -- *And I saw another mighty angel come down from heaven, clothed with a cloud: and a rainbow was upon his head, and his face was as it were the sun, and his feet as pillars of fire: ² And he had in his hand a little book open: and he set his right foot upon the sea, and his left foot on the earth,*

³ And cried with a loud voice, as when a lion roareth: and when he had cried, seven thunders uttered their voices.

So What/Who does these SEVEN Thunders that speaks represents?

Job 37:1-5 -- *At this also my heart trembleth, and is moved out of his place. ² Hear attentively the noise of his voice, and the sound that goeth out of his mouth. ³ He directeth it under the whole heaven, and his lightning unto the ends of the earth. ⁴ After it a voice roareth: he thundereth with the voice of his Excellency; and he will not stay them when his voice is heard. ⁵ **God thundereth marvellously with his voice;** great things doeth he, which we cannot comprehend.*

God thunders with His voice.

John 12:20-29
And there were certain Greeks among them that came up to worship at the feast: ²¹ The same came therefore to Philip, which was of Bethsaida of Galilee, and desired him, saying, Sir, we would see Jesus. ²² Philip cometh and telleth Andrew: and again Andrew and Philip tell

Jesus. ²³ And Jesus answered them, saying, The hour is come, that the Son of man should be glorified. ²⁴ Verily, verily, I say unto you, Except a corn of wheat fall into the ground and die, it abideth alone: but if it die, it bringeth forth much fruit.

²⁵ He that loveth his life shall lose it; and he that hateth his life in this world shall keep it unto life eternal. ²⁶ If any man serve me, let him follow me; and where I am, there shall also my servant be: if any man serve me, him will my Father honour.

*²⁷ Now is my soul troubled; and what shall I say? Father, save me from this hour: but for this cause came I unto this hour. ²⁸ Father, glorify thy name. Then came there a voice from heaven, saying, I have both glorified it, and will glorify it again. ²⁹ The people therefore, that stood by, and heard it, **said that it thundered: others said, An angel spake to him.***

The SEVEN THUNDERS that was uttered represents the seven attributes of the voice of God. We must know these seven attributes before we can speak accurately to the nations and possess the marketplace.

7 Attributes of the Voice of God.

Psalm 29:1-10

Give unto the LORD, O ye mighty, give unto the LORD glory and strength. ² Give unto the LORD the glory due unto his name; worship the LORD in the beauty of holiness. ³ The voice of the LORD is upon the waters: the God of glory thundereth: the LORD is upon many waters. ⁴ The voice of the LORD is powerful; the voice of the LORD is full of majesty. ⁵ The voice of the LORD breaketh the cedars; yea, the LORD breaketh the cedars of Lebanon. ⁶ He maketh them also to skip like a calf; Lebanon and Sirion like a young unicorn. ⁷ The voice of the LORD divideth the flames of fire.

⁸ The voice of the LORD shaketh the wilderness; the LORD shaketh the wilderness of Kadesh. ⁹ The voice of the LORD maketh the hinds to calve (Deer to give birth), and discovereth the forests (Strips the forest bare): and in his temple doth every one speak of his glory. ¹⁰ The LORD sitteth upon the flood; yea, the LORD sitteth King for ever.

To make it clearer to you, I have noted below the seven attributes as contained in the above scripture.

THE SEVEN ATTRIBUTES

#1: Verse 4 - The voice of the LORD is **Powerful**.

#2: Verse 4 - the voice of the LORD is **full of majesty**. His voice rules and reign.

#3: Verse 5&6 - The voice of the LORD **breaketh the cedars** (Nations of the Earth); yea, the LORD breaketh the cedars of Lebanon. He makes them also to skip like a calf; Lebanon and Sirion like a young unicorn.

#4: Verse 7 - The voice of the LORD **divideth the flames of fire**. (Like the day of Pentecost).

#5: Verse 8 - The voice of the LORD **shaketh the wilderness**; the LORD shaketh the wilderness of Kadesh.

#6: Verse 9a - The voice of the LORD **maketh the hinds to calve** (*Deer to give birth*).

#7: Verse 9b - The voice of the Lord **discovereth the forests** (*Strips the forest bare):* and in his temple doth every one speak of his glory.

These 7 attributes equate to the 7 Mountains of Culture that must be conquered for the reclaim of the marketplace to be complete. In my book "Breakthrough Strategies for Christians in the Marketplace, I explain in over 400 pages how we can dominate and reclaim the marketplace as the Lord declared. I will advise you to get a copy of that book for an in-depth study of these breakthrough strategies.

So the purpose of financial reward is to equip you to reclaim the marketplace and make the kingdoms of this world bow to the authority of the kingdom of our God. Praise God. It is not for your personal benefit; but for kingdom purpose; to extend the frontiers of the kingdom of God.

Power and Authority

"Then He called His twelve disciples together and gave them power and authority over all devils, and to cure diseases". (Luke 9:1)

Authority and power are two different things. Your AUTHORITY over the enemy comes through Jesus Christ and your position in Him as a believer. Your POWER over the enemy comes through the Holy Spirit:

And behold, I send the promise of My Father upon you; but tarry ye in the city of Jerusalem, until ye be endued with power from on high. (Luke 24:49)

You must have both authority and power to be effective. Believers receive authority through the new birth experience and their position in Christ. Some never go on to receive the power of the Holy Spirit, which is to be combined with the authority, for effective warfare. Fasting is an essential way to increase your sensitivity to the Holy Spirit and increase his POWER in your life.

So as I end this book, I need you to understand that God has not called us to serve Him in vain. He is a rewarder. But He wants us prepared for the attack of the devourer; so that we can maintain what we have received.

With your giving, your praying and your fasting; you can wage a good warfare and be the best God want you to be. God bless you. See you at the top.

Notes

Other books by Charles Omole

1. **Church, Its time to Fly** -- *Learning to fly on Eagles Wing.*

2. **How to Avoid Getting Hurt in Church** -- *13 Steps that will protect you and help create an atmosphere for breakthroughs.*

3. **Must I go to Church** -- *8 Reasons why you must attend Church.*

4. **Freedom from Condemnation** -- *Breaking free from the burden & weight of sin.*

5. **I cannot serve a big God and remain small**

6. **How to start your own business**

7. **How to Make Godly Decisions**

8. **How to avoid financial collapse**

9. **Let Brotherly love continue: *An insight into love and companionship.***

10. **Breaking out of the debt trap**

11. **Common Causes of Unanswered Prayer.**

12.**How to Argue with God and Win** -- *Biblical strategies on getting God's attention for all your circumstances all of the time*

13.**Avoiding Power Failure** - *How to generate spiritual power for daily success and victorious living.*

14.**How long should I continue to pray when I don't see an answer**?

15. **SUCCESS KILLERS: *Seven Habits of Highly Ineffective Christians*.**

16.**The Financial Resource Handbook** – UK Edition

17.**Divine Strategies for uncommon breakthroughs:** *Living **in the Reality of the Supernatural***:

18.**Keys to Divine Success**

19.**Wrong Thoughts, Wrong Emotion and Wrong Living**

20.**Secrets of Biblical Wealth Transfer**

21.**Journey to Fulfillment**

22.**Prosperity Unleashed** – *A Definitive Guide to Biblical Economics*

23. **No More Debt –** *Volume 1*

24. **Understanding Dominion**

25. **Advancement**

26. **Getting the Story Straight**

27. **Overcoming when Overwhelmed**

28. **The Spiritual Fitness Plan**

29. **Spiritual and Practical Steps to Command Value**

30. **Breakthrough Strategies for Christians in the Marketplace**

For more information about our ministry, world outreaches and a free catalogue of our media and study materials, please write to:

Winning Faith Outreach Ministries
151 Mackenzie Road
London. N7 8NF, UNITED KINGDOM

www.charlesomole.com

Email: info@Charlesomole.com

Notes

Notes

BOOK SUMMARY

There are two systems in operation on Earth: The Kingdom of the World system and the Kingdom of God System – *God's ways of doing things.* So the battle is between the world system and the kingdom of God system. But Satan is the ruler of the darkness of this world In order to rule; he (Satan) had to put in place a System that he can control and that can guarantee his outcome.

Built within that World System is a reward structure that only favour those that serve Satan. The World system was not intended to advance God's purpose but that of Satan. Therefore; anyone serving God's purpose CANNOT benefit from the World's System Satan has set up.

God has a prescribed system of operation for those who are saved, which is greater and better than the world's. Embedded within this system is a financial reward system that is unique to believers in Christ Jesus. How to access this financial reward system is what this book is about. And like any true spiritual principle; I have spent the earlier chapters laying vital foundations that will guide your understanding. These foundations may seem like digression on my part; but they are necessary and I will encourage you to patiently follow the sequence of topical revelation as laid out in this book. Believers must change systems and become educated in the Word of God to learn how to operate in His Kingdom. Many Christians are trying to live according to the world system when they should be operating in the kingdom of God system. This has led to many being controlled by Mammon.

This book goes behind the scene to reveal the spiritual strategy and steps needed to enjoy financial reward from God. The book reveals the essential pillars of the spiritual system that release financial reward. If you have ever sowed seed and not received any harvest yet. If you say, where is my harvest? If you have been faithful giver, tither and yet still live in poverty or lack; then this book is for you. It will answer all these questions and show you how you can command your harvest to manifest by building a superior infrastructure in the spirit.